RIDDLES FOR KIDS 2

OVER 300 RIDDLES AND JOKES FOR CHILDREN

M. PREFONTAINE

D1189179

Published by MP Publishing
Copyright © 2016

What must be broken before it can be used?

Answer: An egg

How do you get a tissue to dance?

Answer: Put a little boogie in it

What stays hot in the refrigerator?

Answer: Mustard

What lives in the ocean, has eight legs and is quick on the draw?

Answer: Billy the squid

What did the outlaw get when he stole a calendar?

Answer: 12 months

What goes through a door but never goes in or comes out?

Answer: A keyhole

What always sleeps with its shoes on?

Answer: A horse

What is the easiest way to double your money?

Answer: Put it in front of the mirror

What was T. rex's favorite number?

Answer: Eight

It stands on one leg with its heart in its head. What is it?

Answer: A cabbage

What is the hardest key to turn?

Answer: A don-key

What do you call a dinosaur with one leg?

Answer: Eileen

Why isn't your nose twelve inches long?

Answer: Because then it would be your foot

Which letter of the alphabet has the most water?

Answer: C

When does Christmas come before Thanksgiving?

Answer: In the dictionary

What is the difference between a jeweler and a jailer?

Answer: A jeweler sells watches and a jailer watches cells

What time is it when 10 elephants are chasing you?

Answer: Ten to one

What falls but never breaks

Answer: nightfall

I can be cracked, I can be made. I can be told, I can be played. What am I?

Answer: A joke

Which word in the dictionary is spelled incorrectly?

Answer: Incorrectly

A slender body, a tiny eye, no matter what happens, I never cry. What am I?

Answer: A needle

What's the difference between a piano and a fish?

Answer: You can tune a piano, but you can't tuna fish

How can you leave a room with two legs and return with six legs?

Answer: Bring a chair back with you

Why didn't the butterfly go to the dance?

Answer: Because it was a moth ball

In a one-story pink house, there was a pink person, a pink cat, a pink fish, a pink computer, a pink chair, a pink table, a pink telephone, a pink shower–everything was pink. What color were the stairs?

Answer: There weren't any stairs, it was a one story house.

What happens when a frog parks in a no-parking space?

Answer: It gets toad away

Why did the woman wear a helmet at the dinner table?

Answer: Because of her crash diet

Why didn't the hot dog star in the movies?

Answer: The roll wasn't good enough

What is snake's favorite subject?

Answer: Hiss-tory

What has hands but cannot clap?

Answer: A clock.

Why did the pony cough?

Answer: He was a little horse

What is as big as an elephant, but weighs nothing at all?

Answer: An elephant's shadow

What key won't open any door?

Answer: A turkey

What type of horses only go out at night?

Answer: Nightmares

Why couldn't the sailors play cards?

Answer: The captain was standing on the deck

What do you call it when two mice almost collide?

Answer: A narrow squeak

When is a black dog not a black dog?

Answer: When it's a grey-hound

A girl is sitting in a house at night that has no lights on at all. There is no lamp, no candle, nothing. Yet she is reading. How?

Answer: The woman is blind and is reading braille.

What goes through towns and over hills but never moves?

Answer: A road

Why didn't the teddy bear eat his lunch?

Answer: Because he was stuffed

What has many rings, but no fingers?

Answer: A telephone

What do you call a shoe made from a banana?

Answer: A slipper

What do elves do after school?

Answer: Gnomework

Why was the baby ant confused?

Answer: Because all his uncles were ants

Name four days of the week that start with the letter "t"?

Answer: Tuesday, Thursday, today, and tomorrow.

What do you call a funny book about eggs?

Answer: Yolk book

How many skunks does it take to stink up a house?

Answer: A phew

You can break me easily without even touching me or seeing me. What am I?

Answer: A promise

What do you get when you cross a walrus with a bee?

Answer: A wallaby

Why was the nose so tired?

Answer: Because it had been running all day

What goes around and around the wood but never goes into the wood?

Answer: The bark on a tree.

How do you make a strawberry shake?

Answer: Tell it a scary story

Why can't a leopard hide?

Answer: Because it's always spotted

It has four eyes but cannot see? What is it?

Answer: Mississippi

What did the beach say when the tide came in?

Answer: Long time no sea

Why couldn't the church steeple keep a secret?

Answer: Because the bell always tolled

What begins with a P and ends with an E and has thousands of letters?

Answer: The Post Office

What animal cheats at exams?

Answer: The cheetah

A man was outside taking a walk, when it started to rain. The man didn't have an umbrella and he wasn't wearing a hat. His clothes got soaked, yet not a single hair on his head got wet. How could this happen?

Answer: The man was bald.

People buy me to eat, but never eat me. What am I?

Answer: A plate

How do bees get to school?

Answer: By the school buzz

Who was the meanest goat in the Wild West?

Answer: Billy the Kid

What kind of vegetable is unpopular on-board ships?

Answer: A leek

What did the cat have for breakfast?

Answer: Mice Crispies

Why did the boy bury his flashlight?

Answer: Because the battery died

What islands should have good singers?

Answer: The Canary Islands

When is a car, not a car?

Answer: When it turns into a parking lot

Why did the outlaw hold up the bakery?

Answer: He kneaded the dough

What does a mixed-up hen lay?

Answer: Scrambled eggs

If everyone bought a red car what would we have?

Answer: A red carnation

What ship has two mates but no captain?

Answer: A relationship

What do you call a cow that plays a musical instrument?

Answer: A Moo-sician

Why are 1999 ten pound notes worth more than 1993 ten pound notes?

Answer: Because there are more of them

What do people make that you can't see?

Answer: Noise

On a fine sunny day, a ship was in the harbor. All of a sudden, the ship began to sink. There was no storm and nothing wrong with the ship yet it sank right in front of the spectator's eyes.
What caused the ship to sink?

Answer: It was a submarine

People from which country are always in a hurry?

Answer: Russians

What has two heads, four eyes, six legs, and a tail?

Answer: A cowboy riding his horse

What do you call a fairy that has not taken a bath?

Answer: Stinky Bell

What do you call a sleeping bull?

Answer: A bulldozer

What kind of water can't freeze?

Answer: Hot water

What kind of star wears sunglasses?

Answer: A movie star

What 4-letter word can be written forward, backward or upside down, and can still be read from left to right?

Answer: Noon

What do you call cattle with a sense of humor?

Answer: Laughing stock

In what place did the rooster crow when all the world heard him?

Answer: In Noah's Ark

What sort of trees come in twos?

Answer: Pear trees

What type of tree can you hold in your hand?

Answer: A palm tree

I am a word. If you pronounce me rightly, it will be wrong. If you pronounce me wrong it is right. What word am I?

Answer: Wrong

What is black, white, and pink all over?

Answer: An embarrassed zebra

Where do rivers sleep?

Answer: In river beds

Why is an island like the letter 'T'?

Answer: Because they are both in the middle of water

How can a pants pockets be empty but still have something in them?

Answer: They have a hole

It flies around all day but never goes anywhere. What is it?

When will water stop running downhill?

Answer: When it reaches the bottom

How do pigs write?

Answer: With a pigpen

What has forty feet and sings?

Answer: The school choir

What is it that you can't hold for more than a few seconds?

Answer: Your breath

What do you get when you cross an automobile with a household animal?

Answer: A carpet

What is round as a dishpan and no matter the size, all the water in the ocean can't fill it up?

Answer: A sieve

What can run but can't walk?

Answer: Water

What does a snowman like to eat for breakfast.

Answer: Frosties

Do rabbits use combs?

Answer: No, they use hare brushes

What kind of coach has no wheels?

Answer: A football coach

Which people like the end of a film?

Answer: The Finnish

What did Mrs. Claus say to Santa when she looked up in the sky?

Answer: Looks like rain dear

What kind of bulbs don't need water?

Answer: Light bulbs

What's a lifeguard's favorite game?

Answer: Pool

What did Tennessee?

Answer: He saw what Arkansas

What has wheels and flies, but it is not an aircraft?

Answer: A garbage truck

What kind of nut has no shell?

Answer: A Doughnut

Look in my face, I am somebody; Look in my back, I am nobody.
What am I?

Answer: I am a mirror

I have a heart that never beats, I have a home but I never sleep. I can take a man's house and build another's, And I love to play games with my many brothers. I am a king among fools. Who am I?

Answer: The King of Hearts in a deck of cards

How do you spell candy in 2 letters?

Answer: c and y c(and)y

What kind of apple isn't an apple?

Answer: A pineapple

Always in you, sometimes on you, if I surround you, I can kill you.

What am I?

Answer: Water

Why are elephants so smart?

Answer: Because they have lots of gray matter

What are moving left to right, right now?

Answer: Your eyes

Which is the oldest tree?

Answer: The elder

The more you take, the more you leave behind. What am I?

Answer: Footsteps

What wears shoes but has no feet?

Answer: The pavement/sidewalk

How can you tell which end of a worm is its head?

Answer: Tickle it in the middle and see which end laughs

How do you make a venomous snake cry?

Answer: Take away its rattle

What would you get if you crossed a rabbit and a lawn sprinkler?

Answer: A hare spray

Re-arrange the letters,
O O U S W T D N E J R
to spell just one word.

Answer: 'just one word'

What has six faces, but does not wear makeup. It also has twenty-one eyes, but cannot see?

Answer: A die (dice)

I am taken from a mine, and shut up in a wooden case, from which I am never released, and yet I am used by almost everybody.

Answer: Pencil lead

What is more useful when it is broken?

Answer: An egg

They have not flesh, nor feathers, nor scales, nor bone. Yet they have fingers and thumbs of their own. What are they?

Answer: Gloves

When can you add two to eleven and get one as the correct answer?

Answer: When you add two hours to eleven o'clock, you get one o'clock

What 7 letter word is spelled the same way backwards and forewords?

Answer: Racecar

Why did the clock get arrested?

Answer: Because it struck twelve

Why was the picture sent to jail?

Answer: Because it was framed?

Imagine you are in a dark room. How do you get out?

Answer: Stop Imagining

I can't be bought but can be stolen with a glance, I'm worthless to one but priceless to two. What am I?

Answer: Love

What temperature does ice freeze at?

Answer: Ice doesn't freeze, it's already frozen

If you eat me, my sender will eat you.
What am I?

Answer: A fish hook

What gets dirtier the more you wash?

Answer: Water

I can be green, black, or even sweet. 2.
It sounds like a letter. What is it?

Answer: Tea

Why are outlaws the strongest men in
the Old West?

Answer: Because they could hold up trains

Why was Cinderella bad at sports?

*Answer: Because she had a pumpkin as a coach, and ran
away from the ball*

Where do sheep get a haircut?

Answer: The baa-baa shop

What bow has no string?

Answer: A rainbow

Why do black sheep eat less than white sheep?

Answer: Because there are less black sheep in the world than white

Why did the chicken cross the road twice, and jump in mud?

Answer: He was a dirty double crosser

A person gets up 180 times every night and sleeps for at least 7 hours at a time. Where does the person live?

Answer: At the North or South Pole

Lighter than air, I float away, with one touch I am destroyed. What am I?

Answer: A bubble

What two whole, positive numbers that have a one-digit answer when multiplied and a two-digit answer when added?

Answer:1 and 9.

I am something that you can you read but not see. I'm with you all the time but sometimes I'm hard to find. What am I?

Answer: Time

How can you hold a piece of string, one end in each hand, and tie a knot in the string without letting go of either end?

Answer: Cross your arms before you seize the ends of the string. Uncross your arms and it will tie a knot

What wears a coat all year-round?

Answer: A dog

I am in your eye. I am a school child. I am a word of five. What am I?

Answer: Pupil

Where do frogs sit?

Answer: On toadstools

I am gentle enough to soothe your skin, light enough to fly in the sky, strong enough to crack rocks. What am I?

Answer: I'm water

What's a pizzas favorite game?

Answer: Dominos

Why are teddy bears never hungry?

Answer: Because they are stuffed

Why can't you play hide-n-seek with chicklets?

Answer: They're always peeping

Why shouldn't you tell a pig a secret?

Answer: Because he is a squealer

I howl, yet I have no voice. Can't be seen but my presence is felt. What am I?

Answer: The wind

What has six legs but only walks with four?

Answer: A horse and rider

A man was walking on a beach, but when he turned around, he saw no footsteps. How is this possible?

Answer: He was walking backwards

I am a three letter word. If you take two letters from me, I am still the same. What word am I?

Answer: The word pea

What is a cow`s favorite game to play at parties?

Answer: Moo-sical chairs

What's nowhere, but everywhere except where something is?

Answer: Nothing

What word does not belong in this list: hold, told, scold, gold, or mold?

Answer: Or

What is not dry nor wet but can be both?

Answer: Ice

What lives in winter, dies in summer, and grows with its roots upward?

Answer: An icicle

A duck arrives near a lake. He sees a sign were it is written "No swimming allowed.", but the duck jumps into the water. Why?

Answer: Because ducks can't read

What has a heart but no other organs?

Answer: A deck of cards

I am a king who measures things. What am I?

Answer: A ruler

Three times what number is no larger than two times the same number?

Answer: 0

What can be seen in the middle of March and April that cannot be seen at the beginning or end of either month?

Answer: The letter 'r'

What house can fly?

Answer: Housefly

It doesn't bark, it doesn't bite but it still won't let you in the house. What is it?

Answer: A lock

When I take 5 and add 6, I get 11. But when I add 6 and 7, I get 1. What am I?

Answer: A clock

What do you get when you cross a roach and a rabbit?

Answer: Bugs Bunny

What do you call a flying monkey?

Answer: A hot air baboon

If 1 equals 5, 2 equals 10, 3 equals 15, 4 equals 20, then what does 5 equals to?

Answer: 1 -- because 1 equals 5

What flies without wings?

Answer: Time

What is the best day to go to the beach?

Answer: A Sunday

What would you get if 120 rabbits took one step backwards at the same time?

Answer: A receding hair line

What do you buy but you never keep?

Answer: Food

I am a type of room you cannot enter or leave. Raised from the ground below, I could be poisonous or a delicious treat. What am I?

Answer: Mushroom

What's 3/7 chicken, 2/3 cat, and 2/4 goat?

Answer: Chicago

What do you call something with no body and no nose?

Answer: Nobody knows

What has 22 legs and 2 wings?

Answer: A football team

What is drawn by everyone without using a pen or pencil?

Answer Breath

When the dog sat on some sandpaper what did he say?

Answer: Ruff

The part of the bird that is not the sky, which can swim in the ocean and always stay dry. What is it?

Answer: The bird's shadow

What type of house weighs the least?

Answer: A lighthouse

Why are giraffes so slow to apologize?

Answer: It takes a long time for them to swallow their pride

If there are four sheep, two dogs and one herds-men, how many feet are there?

Answer: Two. Sheep have hooves; dogs have paws; only people have feet

Everyone can hold me, but not in there hand, and not forever. What am I?

Answer: Your breath

Who does the ocean date?

Answer: It goes out with the tide

What starts with E ends with E and has one letter in it?

Answer: An envelope

If you have three you have three, if you have two you have two and if you have one you have none. What am I?

Answer: Choices

Three doctors say Robert is their brother. However, Robert says he has no brother. Who's lying?

Answer: No one. The doctors are all girls

Who is never hungry during Christmas?

Answer: The turkey because he is always stuffed

What do you call a person who is afraid of Santa Claus?

Answer: Claustraophobic

If Theresa's daughter is my daughter's mother, what am I to Theresa?

Answer: Theresa's Daughter

Why are Christmas trees bad at knitting?

Answer: Because they always drop their needles

What has no beginning, no end, and nothing in the middle?

Answer: A donut

What do you call seaside spooks?

Answer: Ghost guards

What do farmers and gardeners grow at the same time?

Answer: Older

What is the difference between a forged dollar note and an insane rabbit?

Answer: One is bad money and the other is a mad bunny

I have two coins, one is marked George I and one is marked George IV. One is genuine but one is a forgery. Which is the forgery?

Answer: George I. A coin would not be marked George I because at the time it was produced it would not have been known that there was going to be a George II

How do spiders communicate?

Answer: Through the world wide web

How can you take 2 from 5 and leave 4?

Answer: F I V E. Remove the 2 letters F and E from five and you have IV

What do you get when you cross a black cat and a lemon?

Answer: A Sour Puss

Who was the the most famous Skeleton detective?

Answer: Sherlock Bones

Why didn't the Mummy have any friends?

Answer: He was too wrapped up in himself

Which part of a road do Ghost's love to travel the most?

Answer: The Dead End

I shrink smaller every time I take a bath. What am I?

Answer: Soap

What did the antelope say when he read the newspaper?

Answer: That's gnus to me.

Which jungle animal is the best dresser?

Answer: The dandy lion

I am a word of six; my first three letters refer to an automobile; my last three letters refer to a household animal; my first four letters is a fish; my whole is found in your room. What am I?

Answer: A carpet

What is faster hot or cold?

Answer: Hot, you can easily catch a cold

I grow in the dark and shine in the light;
The paler I am, the more I am liked;
My maker never gets paid, but never goes on strike.
What am I?

Answer: A pearl

The Bay of Bengal is in which state?

Answer: Liquid

Why didn't the monster eat the crazy person?

Answer: He was allergic to nuts

Why did Snap, Crackle and Pop get scared?

Answer: They heard there was a cereal killer on the loose

I turn around once. What is out will not get in. I turn around again. What is in will not get out. What am I?

Answer: A key

What star slept for 100 years?

Answer: Rip Van Twinkle

What did the mother kangaroo give birth to?

Answer: A bouncing baby

What do people spend a lot of money on every year but never want to use?

Answer: Insurance

Why was the chef embarrassed?

Answer: Because he saw the salad dressing

Which is the most curious letter?

Answer: Y?

What instrument can you hear but never see?

Answer: Your voice

What is the best month for a parade?

Answer: March

How do you stop a wild boar charging?

Answer: Take away its credit card

Who helped the werewolf go to the ball?

Answer: Its hairy godmother

What two ton animal can put you in a trance?

Answer: A hypnopottamus

What do jigsaws do when they get unwelcome news?

Answer: Go to pieces

I am white when I am dirty, and black when I am clean. What am I?

Answer: Blackboard

I make two people out of one. What am I?

Answer: A mirror

I have a thousand needles but I do not sew.
What am I?

Answer: A Porcupine

David's father has three sons : Snap, Crackle and _____ ?

Answer: David

I am not alive, but I grow; I don't have lungs, but I need air; I don't have a mouth, but water kills me. What am I?

Answer: Fire

Before Mount Everest was discovered, what was the highest mountain on Earth?

Answer: Mount Everest

When is a doctor most annoyed?

Answer: When he has run out of patients

Why may carpenters reasonably believe there is no such thing as stone?

Answer: Because they never saw it

What lives upon its own substance and dies when it has devoured itself?

Answer: A candle

How do fishermen make their nets?

Answer: They just take a lot of holes and sew them together

I sometimes run, but I cannot walk. You always follow me around. What am I?

Answer: Your Nose

Where do smart dogs refuse to shop?

Answer: At flea markets

Why do tigers eat raw meat?

Answer: Because they are lousy cooks

What animal is the most difficult to understand?

Answer: A mumble bee

If you drop a yellow hat in the Red Sea, what does it become?

Answer: Wet

What did the sea say to the sand?

Answer: Nothing, he just waved

What has words but never speaks?

Answer: A book

What is the greatest worldwide use of cowhide?

Answer: To cover cows

What lies on the ground, a hundred feet in the air?

Answer: A dead centipede

Why do dragons sleep all day?

Answer: They like to hunt Knights

You are my brother, but I am not your brother. Who am I?

Answer: I am your sister

What do trees and dogs have in common.

Answer: bark

Why is a wise man like a pin?

Answer: He has a head and comes to a point

A woman is travelling around London when she passes Trafalgar Square she is sent straight to jail but she has done nothing wrong. Why is this?

Answer: She is playing monopoly

A man is travelling towards the centre of a field; he knows that when he gets there he is going to be badly injured. Why does he know this?

Answer: He has jumped from an aeroplane and his parachute has failed to open

I have all the knowledge you have. But I am small as your fist that your hands can hold me. Who am I?

Answer: I am your Brain

What do you put on top of a doghouse?

Answer: A woof

What did the doctor say to the invisible man?

Answer: I'm sorry, you'll have to come back later. I can't see you right now

What is a shark's favorite game?

Answer: Swallow the leader

How do you make a lemon drop?

Answer: You let it go

What state has a friendly greeting for everyone?

Answer: Ohio

What do you get when you mix SpongeBob with Albert Einstein?

Answer: Sponge Bob Smarty Pants

Who is the tallest Jedi?

Answer: Luke Skyscraper

What does a dog do that people step in?

Answer: Pants

What do you call a musical insect?

Answer: A humbug

What would you get if you crossed a birthday cake and an earthquake?

Answer: Crumbs

What do you do when you see a kidnapping in the park?

Answer: Wake him up

I'm at the beginning of eternity and the end of time and space. What am I?

Answer: The letter E

What do you call a 100-year-old ant?

Answer: ANT-ique

What do you call a train full of bubble gum?

Answer: A chew-chew train

What did the judge say when the skunk entered the court?

Answer: "Odour in the court"

What do you call a fly with no wings?

Answer: A walk

Hat animal makes the most of its food?

Answer: A giraffe. They make it go a long way

How do rabbits travel?

Answer: By hareplane

What is dirty after washing?

Answer: Your bath water

Do you know what you can hold without ever touching it?

Answer: A conversation.

What has two legs but cannot walk?

Answer: A pair of trousers

What falls but is never injured?

Answer: The rain

What has three ways out and just one way in?

Answer: A T-shirt

When can a man walk on water?

Answer: When the water freezes

What insect gets 'As' in English?

Answer: A spelling bee

What is the first thing you do in the
morning?

Answer: You wake up

Where can you always find money

Answer: In the dictionary

Who has friends for lunch?

Answer: A cannibal

What cat lives in the ocean?

Answer: An octopus

What time is the same spelt forwards or
backwards?

Answer: Noon

Which lion is a very good swimmer?

Answer: The sea-lion

Why did the outlaw hold up the river?

Answer: Because they heard it had two banks

Why are Saturday and Sunday stronger than the rest of the week?

Answer: Because the rest are weak days

Is it hard to spot a leopard?

Answer: No they come that way

What is the difference between a bottle of medicine and a doormat?

Answer: One is shaken up and taken the other is taken up and shaken

What goes to bed with its shoes on?

Answer: A horse

What looks like half a tomato?

Answer: The other half

Which fish is also a weapon?

Answer: A swordfish

What becomes smaller when you turn it upside down?

Answer: The number 9

Why did the Sheriff arrest the chicken?

Answer: Because it used fowl language

What do you get if you feed a lemon to a cat?

Answer: A sourpuss

How many types of gnu are there?

Answer: Two. Good gnus and bad gnus

25278800R00033

Printed in Great Britain
by Amazon